IMPACT BIBLE ACADEMY
STUDENT'S LEADERS MANUAL

BIBLICAL INSIGHT
(Section One)

Dr. Eugenia Gumm
Elder Charles R. Byrd

© 2022 by Dr. Eugenia Gumm and Elder Charles Byrd

All rights are reserved. No part of this publication may be reprinted or reproduced for commercial or profit purposes without written permission of the publisher and Authors.

All scriptures are taken from the King James Version of the Bible. All references listed have been used by permission.

Images used are Royalty free.

ISBN: 978-1-7335430-5-7

Editor: Renee Gray-Crutcher

Cover Designer: Redlifecreative.com

Publisher MWOGM
PO Box 0623
Dayton, Ohio 45401-0623

Printed in the United States of America

Disclaimer – Our views only reflect our beliefs, not reflective of any denomination, or their religious beliefs.

ACKNOWLEDGEMENTS

Giving Honor to our Lord and Savior Jesus Christ who is truly above all!

Giving Special Thanks to Elder Charles Byrd, along with his beautiful wife Evangelist Ruby Byrd, for joining our team and assisting individuals with their Growth in God.

I truly and gratefully appreciate my Overseer Apostle Connie L. Bogus, Jr. and Precious wife Evangelist. Shirley Bogus, for all you had done for me, especially Praying.

I am Indebted to Bishop Dr. Ronald Southhall for giving me the opportunity to grow and expand with Agape Love Institution located in Texas and Professor Marshall Howard from Indianapolis, Indiana. Both of you are a Mighty Blessing to me and others in the body of Christ.

I am overly Thankful for one of my Mentor Tina Toles who is President of the Dayton Christian Writer's Guild, for her encouraging Words and assisting me to become an Author. Furthermore, I appreciate all the members of the Dayton Christian Writer's Guild for being there for me.

Renee Gray-Crutcher you are Outstanding and I totally Appreciate you for All you have done for me with my publishing endeavors. You are One of a Kind.

Prophetess Evangelist Vita Shield Wow! You are the Best and I Value all of your labor you do for me. You are Greatly Cherish.

I am pleased, in which, my three adult children keep showing me the reason for Developing this course. I Love you all and I Truly Thank God for you all! You keep me in the Face of God, Always!

Thank you Mom for your Inspiring Words of Love, you had always given me over the years.

To all my Sisters and Brothers (James, Susan, Antonia, Gwendolyn, and Jacqueline) for letting me know I can do it, just put my mind to it.

Last and not least, Words cannot express how I am overwhelmed with Gratification for the Good Lord Above placing my Armour Bearer Prophetess Sharon E. Lockett in my Life, for such a Time as This.   ***Truly you are a Trooper!***

Dr. Eugenia Gumm

ACKNOWLEDGEMENTS

To Our Lord and Savior for the experiences and teaching He has given me all my life, and the Blessings that has been life changing and everlasting.

To My Loving Wife Ruby who has been with me and supported me down through the years.

To Dr. Eugenia Gumm for this awesome opportunity to teach others and to affirm the knowledge I have and will continue to inquire in the future.

Elder Charles Byrd

Contents

ACKNOWLEDGEMENTS i
ACKNOWLEDGEMENTS iii
FORWARD.. vii
INTRODUCTION ix
TIME WITH GOD 1
KNOW THE BIBLE (Part One) 13
KNOW THE BIBLE (Part Two) 39
REVIEW OF MINI-TERM 51
DISCIPLINE POSITION 53
PROTOCOL 63
CEREMONIES 71
REVIEW FINAL TEST 87
REFERENCES 89

FORWARD

The creation of this Instructor's Manual has been a labor of love. Developed for students who will become instructors and leaders for the next generation. Dr Eugenia Gumm and Elder Charles Byrd have diligently worked on the curriculum placed within this manual. Their dedication and commitment is in each page.

Please make this your resource to increase your knowledge, so you can inspire next level outcome in others.

What a pleasure it has been to work with Dr Gumm for the past few years. This particular project has taken time, research and love to complete for you.

Happy Studying.

Renee Gray-Crutcher
Editor

INTRODUCTION

"Study to show thyself approved unto God, a workman that needeth not to be ashamed, righty dividing the word of truth."   II Timothy 2:15

In both as a Leader in the Kingdom of God, as well as, a member in the Kingdom of God, one must always understand and know His Word, and how to apply it in this pilgrimage life.

We hope to teach His Word and apply its meaning with divine principals that will enhance one's ability to achieve eternal life.

When a person has accepted Jesus Christ as their Lord and Savior and being new to the body of Christ. One must expect more than just coming to Him, of course there is some excitement at first. In addition, the question is how long the excitement will last?

For instance, if a person isn't growing in Christ their life would become stagnated (past tense) cease to flow or move; or better yet cease developing; become inactive or dull.

The contents in this book is formulated for the purpose of the Instructors to have the autonomy to expound as deeply as they see fit.

One of the main reasons for this Training Manuel is to assist individuals with their Development in Christ, as well as, to know who they are and to walk in their God given Divine Calling. To fully know God is to Love Him.

PROJECT I (Introduction Test)

Fully knowing God is to Love Him,

Vessels of the Almighty God,

Dr. Eugenia Gumm

Elder Charles Byrd

Dr. Eugenia Gumm & Elder Charles R. Byrd

TIME WITH GOD

Time with God is one of the greatest experiences one could have. Looking at it this way, in order, to learn or know someone or something, you have to spend time with him/her/or it.

When you don't spend time with him/her/or it, how can you say you know the individual or the thing you may need to know or learn for your life.

In this day and time, it is Crucial for one to become a Scholar at learning and knowing the Word of God, which is the Holy Bible. By doing this you will experience the fullness of His Glory! In ways you may not be able to explain.

The more you devote yourself to God the more you will be increased in Wisdom, Knowledge, and Understanding in Him!

Well let's look at <u>Time</u>:

    1.) <u>Who created time?</u> _____

- _____
- _____

    2.) <u>What is Time?</u> _____

- _____
- _____
- _____
- _____
- _____

3.) Why is Time Important? _____

_____

- _____
- _____

4.) When do we need to Manage Time? _____

_____

- _____
- _____

5.) How do you spend your Time? _____

_____

- _____

As you can see Time is very important and hopefully you do not used your time unwisely.

Getting a little more understanding about the word, the key is "With" when it comes to a Relationship with God (talking with God, on a daily bases):

- _____
- _____
- _____
- _____

(Agree or Agreeing) *Amos 3:3*

- _____
- _____
- _____

- _____
- _____
- _____
- _____

It is clear in order for even two people to walk together they must agree. Better yet, visualizing it this way, by simply being in covenant with someone (Marriage), and especially with God.

Therefore, let's glance at Enoch who walked with God until he was not. He lived 365 years. *Genesis 5:22-24*

Then there is Noah who walked with God. And he lived to be 350 years. *Genesis 6:9*

David who went to the "Cave of Adullam" and spent time there hiding from King Saul, who wanted to kill him. During the time he was in the cave he wrote several Psalms, which shows us his relationship with God. *Psalms 57*; *1 Samuel 22*

It is a journey walking with God; learning how to Trust, Engage, and Loving Him fully.

- <u>Trust</u> _____
  _____
  _____

- <u>Engage</u> _____
  _____
  _____

- <u>Loving</u> _____
  _____

_____

When you look at it this way, your walk with Him can become more fulfilling to you in every way.

God is our Supreme Being of all Creation including Mankind. _____

Truly, He is the first and the last, the beginning and the ending. _____
_____ The Lord is one who is Above All, in All and Through All.
_____

Time with God

Is one of the greatest and most intimate time a person can have with the Supreme Being. Being intimate with someone can get pretty personal to telling your deepest secrets or even dreams, to down to something you wish or have done (And gotten away with).

Intimacy with someone could mean you trust them fully to tell them your thoughts and desires, in which, one is very protected of due to passed hurts, abandonment, rejection which could bring rebellion, most of all broken trust, let alone betrayal.

If you would like or want a more **Immeasurable**, **Internal**, and **Special** Relationship, you must draw closer to Him. By searching the Scriptures "For in them ye think ye have Eternal life, for they testify about me, and me is Christ".   Wow! _____, _____

   (The next chapter "Know **your** Bible", will go in depth about the Bible)

Another way to draw closer to Him is by setting a certain Day and Time to apply oneself to "Time With God".

- _____
- _____
- _____
- _____

An <u>Internal</u> Relationship with God is knowing and walking in His Heartbeat.

- _____
- _____

Furthermore, the Lord of Host is Meek and Lowly in Heart. This is why we must spend time with Him to learn of Him and His Ways. _____
_____

Do you have a <u>Special</u> Relationship with someone, in which, the individual(s) has a place in your heart?

The Living God would like to have a place in our heart for this is the Will of God for us. He wants us to Love Him with All our heart, soul and mind. _____ _____, _____
_____

Even thou God knows all things, He still wants to hear your voice and know you would like to spend time with Him. _____
_____

In addition, you need to talk to Him on a daily basis.

- Prayer is _____

- Prayer is _____

- Prayer _____

- Pray _____

God made us for His Glory! <u>Romans 9:21</u>
"How Marvelous"

In spending Time with God, _____
_____

Our Lord comfort us in times of trouble(s), as He cares for us. Our cares are for us, as well as, for one another. _____

<u>PROJECT 2</u>

1.) Spend _____ hours per day with God in Prayer.

2.) Have a set time _____ to meet God in Prayer _____.

3.) _____ your time you meet with the Almighty.

4.) Make a Prayer List of _____

_____

_____

_____

_____

5.) Make a list of _____

_____

6.) Create a _____

_____

7.) Each week _____

_____

8.) Cares (Different) _____

_____

Supporting Scriptures: _____

_____

_____

Dr. Eugenia Gumm & Elder Charles R. Byrd

Project 3

*Key point: A Leader who took time to Pray & Fast New Testament (NT), for perfect law & mankind.

    (1)   Who was he?

    (2)   Where is the scripture(s)?

    (3)   How important was the situation (Praying & Fasting), toward salvation?

    (4)   How is it going to relate to your Ministry?

Idolatry is _____

_____

- Idolatry: _____
- Idolatry_____
    - ➤ _____

Then saith Jesus _____

_____

_____

Name some things that take you away from the Lord:

<u>(In Class Project)</u>

Believe it or not, this can get between you and God.

These key elements comprise your devotion to God. Your day should be divided up into three equal parts, which are:

- Eight hours for _____

- Eight hours for _____
- Eights for _____

Devotion is _____
_____
_____
_____

Vocation is _____
_____
_____
_____

Relaxation is _____
_____
_____
_____

Once you begin the Quest of knowing God, you will Have an Earthshaking Relationship with Him, in which, you will Never Forget, most of all Cherish Forever.

NOTES

NOTES

Dr. Eugenia Gumm & Elder Charles R. Byrd

KNOW THE BIBLE
(Part One)

How do you know what you know? Simply, by spending time with what you know or who you know. For instance, on the job training, reading, researching a matter or even a situation by going over and over it again. In doing this one would become familiar with a given interest, thing, person, even a group of people.

This is one way to begin to know a subject by listening or training in a school. Meanwhile, to know something is valuable. Especially, when a person applies it to their life.

On the other hand, the Holy Bible which is the Divine Word of God. Which is the book of life for mankind. If one would just read, study, and most of all apply the Word to their life, he/she will live forever.   WOW!!

Lets look at the word:

   KNOW or (K) NOW

    A.) <u>Know-</u> _____

          _____

          _____

    B.) <u>Now-</u> _____

          _____

          _____

There are several reasons why you need to know the Word of God Now. Basically, because of the time period we live in. We live in a time when right is wrong, wrong is right. On the other hand, right is right (If no one is doing it) and wrong is wrong (If everyone is doing it).

Furthermore, there is a great deal of fear, deception, oppression which leads into depression which could bring on suppression and then of course suicide, if a person does not get some kind of help. The Word of the Living God brings, Love, Hope, Encouragement, and Direction, as well as, Correction.

Think of the Word this way (God's Word Is):

Word	Book	Verse
Pure		
Stand		
Seed		
Quick & Powerful		
Born Again		
His Name		
Keepeth His Word		
Dwell Richly		
Cleanse		
Life		
Truth		
Beginning		

By Knowing the Word of God, one can share it by teaching, preaching, and most of all living the Word of God. And demonstrating their love for the God you service.

Are you ready to take a walk through the living Bible from Genesis through Revelation?

Project 4

1.) Know each book of the Bible: Names
2.) Know their meaning
3.) Know their Section of the Bible
4.) Know each book writer
5.) Know each book of the Bible abbreviation

Bonus: Know each Book Time Zone or period

Viewing the _____
of the Holy Word will assist a person in their way of life.

During the time period of 1611 A.D., the King James Version of the Bible was first published. The translation of the Bible was sanction under the auspices of King James the first King of England. And was written in _____
_____
_____

The Bible has two main sections which are _____ and _____ and they consist of _____ books:

Section	Books
Old Testament	
New Testament	
Total	

Testament means _____
_____

    A.)   Covenant _____
_____
_____.

OLD Testament (OT)

Is the first major section of the Bible, known as the _____

_____

_____

Which contains the Books of the _____

_____

_____

Books in the OT:

The books of the _____

_____

_____

_____

Law books consist of the first five books of the Bible written by Moses:

Books	Writer

Biblical Insight – Student's Manual

In this pilgrimage for the Israelites, they were met with antagonistic, as well as, cruel customs and pagan orientated people, which challenge the Word of God. Which brought out the principles of God and its usages.

The _____ OT _____:

Books	Writer

In serving our Lord there are daily questions and inquiries of daily life, in which, you need God's inspiring wisdom, love, suffering, and relationship, which comes about in having a practical and spiritual life with God. The books of _____ are designed to consolidate all manners in one's journey.

Poetry _____

_____. There are <u>five</u>

books which are:

Books	Writer

Major Prophets

Major _____

_____.

Prophet _____

_____.

- _____
- _____
- _____

- _____
- _____
- _____
- _____
- _____
- _____

There are (Four), _____
Prophets:

Name	Meaning	Author

Minor Prophets

Are just as essential as the Major Prophets, it just depend on the time period, in which, they were in.

There are Twelve Minor Prophets:

Name	Meaning	Author

These are the books which make up the Thirty-Nine books of the Old Testament Covenant in the Holy Bible of the Living God.

NEW Testament (NT)

This is an interval phase which is After Christ (AD), in addition to outlining the Life of Christ from His birth to His death on the Cross.

Furthermore, the Highest reason why Christ came to the earth realm and gave up His existence for us on earth, especially our sins, in order, to redeem us back to Him, for the reason the first (Adam) Failed. _____
_____

Therefore, He had to come Himself, to Redeem the World back to Himself _
_____

Truly, By Grace are we Saved _____

The NT consist of Twenty-Seven Books, in which, Apostle Paul who was named Saul had wrote the foremost of the volumes, along with others (See below)

Name	Meaning	Author

Dr. Eugenia Gumm & Elder Charles R. Byrd

Name	Meaning	Author

Biblical Insight – Student's Manual

Name	Meaning	Author

These are the twenty-seven books of the Word of God. In them one would find life everlasting and forever more.

Redemption

- Knowledge and using every Word of the Bible will bring on Redemption.
- Redemption: _____
_____
_____.
- Redemption _____
_____
_____

What can you come in to the World without and What do you need to leave this World with? _

_____

Biblical Insight – Student's Manual

SALVATION
CORRUPTIBLE TO UNCORRUPTIBLE

Renee Gray-Crutcher

SALVATION:

- The Old Covenant: _____
  _____
  _____

- The New Covenant: _____
  _____

  o _____
    _____
    _____
    _____
    _____
    _____

- _____
  _____

- _____
  _____

Salvation _____
_____
_____

When Jesus spoke about Forgiveness, we must forgive Seventy times Seven, basically, until we are "Complete". _____
_____

For God knows what we need to be "Complete" for us to be Saved from the Wrath of God. _____
_____

Project 5

1.) What is Salvation?

2.) Who brought Salvation? Why?

3.) Know the Scriptures for Salvation

4.) Can a person be saved without Salvation?

SEVEN

For as much, looking at the Number Seven being _____
_____
_____

- <u>Hebrew Language</u>: Strong's Concordance (#7651) "Sheh' bah" or "Shib-ah" means: The sacred full one, Seven Times, and a week….

- <u>Greek language</u>: Strong's Concordance (#2033) "Hep-tah'" or "Hepta" means A primary number Seven or Seventh

Looking down through the generation's history until our present time there are Seven Dispensation Period which flows from one generation or generations to another.

Seven Dispensation Periods

The number <u>Seven</u> is very significant, even from the beginning of the creation of heaven and earth. Along with the moving creatures in the waters, furthermore, the fowls of the air, the cattle, creepy things and beast of the earth. Most of all, mankind. God had ended all His Work on the Seventh Day, in which He rested.

For the most part the number Seven is of completion and Power, in which the Living God Had made All Creation, for His Glory! _____
_____

On the other hand, Dispensation is _____

_____

_____

_____

_____

_____

Period, _____

Therefore, What are the Seven Dispensation Periods?

- _____
- _____
- _____
- _____

Dispensation of Innocence 1st

1.) _____

2.) _____

3.) _____

4.) _____

5.) _____

Dispensation of Conscience 2nd _____

_____
_____
_____
_____

Example, _____
_____
_____
_____.

_____
_____
_____

This is just one example where man's consciences have netted him severe consequence, as it relates to God's commands.

Dispensation of Government 3rd _____

_____
_____
_____
_____.
_____
_____
_____

Dispensation of Patriarchal Rule 4th

_____
_____
_____
_____
_____
_____.

Dispensation is Mosaic Law 5th _____

_____
_____
_____
_____.

Dispensation of Grace 6th _____

_____

This "Age of Grace" or Church Age occurs between, the 69th and 70th week of _____. It starts with the coming of the Spirit on the Day of Pentecost and ends with the Rapture of the Church _____ _____.

By the way, the number Six represents Man, which was made on the six day of Creation _____ _____.

Dispensation of Millennial Kingdom 7th

_____

_____

_____.

The only people allowed to enter the Kingdom are the again Believers from the Age of Grace.

1) What is the nature of the Millennium?
2) How will Christ rule in the Millennium?
3) Where will the capital city of the world be during the thousand-year reign of Christ?
4) How will the world be changed during the Millennium?
5) What does the Bible teach about the rebuilding of the temple during the Millennium?

Project 6

1.) Know the meaning of the Dispensation Periods? Why?
2.) Know how many Dispensation Periods there are and their meaning?
3.) Know the Dispensation Periods Scriptures and the generations in them.
4.) What Dispensation Period are we in today?
5.) What is the nature of the Millennium?
6.) How will Christ rule in the Millennium?
7.) Where will the capital city of the world be during the thousand-year reign of Christ?
8.) Where will the world be changed during the Millennium?
9.) What does the Bible teach about the rebuilding of the temple during the Millennium?
    a. Is there a future Dispensation Periods? Why?

Furthermore, looking at the Seven churches in _____
_____, which are very significant to today's Churches.

Upon each Church (which are in Asia) is different in various ways, in which, each one can and should improve if each church would Stop, Look, Listen, and Do/Action!

_____

Biblical Insight – Student's Manual

Project 7

SEVEN CHURCHES:

1.) What are the Seven Churches?
2.) What does the Word say about each Church?
3.) How could each Church represent our present Church today?
4.) Know each Church meaning: Why?
5.) Which Church can you relate to?

CHURCH	STOP	LOOK	LISTEN	Do/ ACTION

We can all learn from these seven churches, in a way we should conduct our lives, especially with other individuals, as well as, behind closed doors. Our life is an open book when it comes to the Living God, who is above all, in all and through all.

Heaven and New Birth Will Begin!

Dr. Eugenia Gumm & Elder Charles R. Byrd

KNOW THE BIBLE
(Part Two)

Have you ever purpose in your mind to read and study the whole Bible? Well, if you have not, you should. The reason is when God has chosen you from the beginning to Salvation and sanction you of His Spirit, in which, He has Called you by His Gospel, to Know the His Word.

_____

By Knowing His Word you would be able to Rightly divide the Word of Truth. _____

Therefore, have you heard of Abraham, Isaac, and Jacob? Wow! If you have Not you are in for a Wonderful Story, in which, our Lord Jesus Christ blood line was from and before all of this Mel-chiz'e-dek King of Salem was the Priest of God of whom Abraham gave Tithes and Mel-chiz'e-dek Blessed Abraham: _____

Name	Meaning	Promise	Begat
Abraham			
Isaac			
Jacob			

Biblical Insight – Student's Manual

These are the generations of Jesus Christ _____
_____, furthermore, look at the children from Jacob which are the twelve Tribes of Israel.

1) Abraham, _____
   _____

   - Abraham wife Sarah _____
     _____
     _____

   - Hagar was _____
     _____
     _____

   - Ishmael: _____
     _____
     _____

2) Isaac _____
   _____
   _____

   - Rebecca _____
     _____
     _____

3) Jacob _____
   _____

- _____
  _____
  _____.

- _____
  _____
  _____.

- _____
  _____
  _____.

- _____
  _____
  _____.

The Twelve Tribes was formed see list and the Supporting scriptures _____
_____

Project 8

1.) Know the twelve tribes?

2.) Know each one mother and father?

3.) Was any of the tribe's mother a concubine? Name them.

4.) Know the meaning of each tribe?

5.) Know the order of each tribe and when born?

6.) Know which tribe was blessed or cursed. Why?

7.) Know the Book and Scriptures they are in?

Twelve Tribes of Israel are as follows:

Name	Meaning	Mother	Cursed or Blessed

As time went on a division came among the Tribes, in which, there was formed the Northern Kingdom, due to King Solomon's successor (his son) Rehoboam who dealt hard with the old men counsel of Israel_____ _____

Kingdom

Northern (___) _____	**Southern (___)** _____
_____	_____
_____	_____
_____	_____
_____	_____
_____	_____

Ishmael _____

_____

_____

_____

_____

Twelve Princes as follows:	_____
	_____
	_____
	_____
	_____
	_____

God was with Ishmael and he becomes Archer (A person who shoots with a bow and arrows). In turn, being father to twelve sons which is referred to the Nomadic Tribes of the Northern Arabia.

The Midianites was formed and basically, joined with the Ishmaelite and lived in the land of Midian Northwestern Arabia which is east of the Gulf of Aqaba.

He was the father _____

Dr. Eugenia Gumm & Elder Charles R. Byrd

Project 9

1.) Who was the Twelve Princes Father?

2.) Who was the Twelve Princes Mother?

3.) Who was the Twelve Princes Grandmother? Know Why?

4.) Who was separated from the original family? And Why?

5.) Name the Twelve Princes in order?

6.) Who are the Twelve Princes descendants?

7.) Who are the Twelve Princes Today?

Kingdom _____

_____.

Greek word for Kingdom "_____

_____".

Primarily "_____".

In addition there are (2) Kingdoms of the Living God which are:

■ The Kingdom of God and of Heaven

    Kingdom of God

- _____
  _____

- _____
  _____

Biblical Insight – Student's Manual

The Kingdom of Heaven

- _____
  _____.

- _____
  _____

TWELVE

Which the governmental perfection and symbolizes God's perfect, divine accomplishment actively manifested. It shows a completeness of a growth or administration.

The number twelve is used _____ in the Bible. Let's look at a few:

- _____
- _____
- _____
- _____
- _____
- _____
- _____
- _____
- _____

Truly, the number Twelve is the main number (Strong's Concordance number 1427) for foundation in the Greek language the word is Dodeka "do-dek-ah" which means: two and ten a dozen which is used frequently in the Gospels for the twelve Apostles, as well as, the Twelve Tribes and relating to Heavenly Jerusalem a Divine Administration in God!!!!!

Furthermore the _____

_____

_____

_____

There are many other events in the Holy Word, regarding the number Twelve which is exciting to read and study about.

Project X

1.) Explain the Twelve Gates of New Jerusalem

2.) Know where the New Jerusalem Gates are found

3.) Explain and name the Twelve Apostles of the Lamb

4.) Explain the Twelve Stones of God, pertaining to Joshua

In the Conclusion we as human beings live with the number Twelve each and every day, hour, months, and year. There are Twelve months which makes up one year. In turn, there are four quarters to one year, which consist of:

Winter	Spring	Summer	Fall

Each day has _____

_____:

- A.M., _____

- P.M., _____.

Since there are twenty-four hours in one day, which can be divided into four parts to an hour, which still has three different times to each segment, for example:

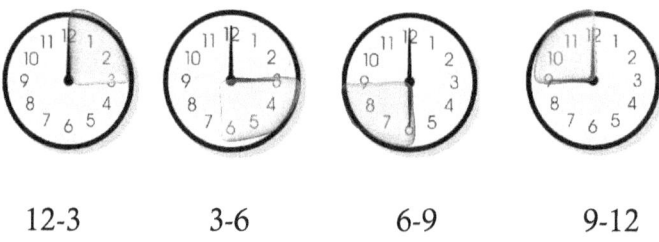

    12-3   3-6   6-9   9-12

Notice the figure of the clock above from:

- Twelve Noon to Eleven Fifty-Nine P.M. (Afternoon to evening to late evening). A total of Twelve Hours

- Twelve Mid-night to eleven Fifty-Nine A.M. (Early Morning to mid-morning to late morning). A total of Twelve Hours

Time: am, pm

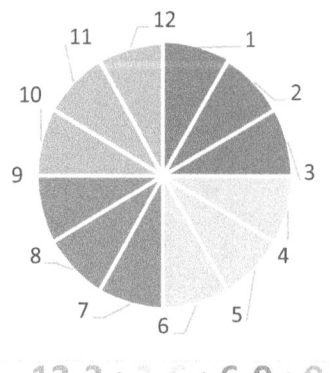

12-3 ; 3-6 ; 6-9 ; 9-12

The number Twelve is broad when we take a look at it from the Bible Perspective. In turn, let's view the number Ten from the Bible point of view. In one aspect looking at the Ten Commandments:

- ❖ _____
- ❖ _____
- ❖ _____
- ❖ _____
- ❖ _____
- ❖ _____
- ❖ _____
- ❖ _____
- ❖ _____
- ❖ _____

The Ten Commandments is part of the Law, which God gave to Moses for our conduct thru everyday life. It tells us how to speak, walk, and act within the confines of the way God's want mankind to live.

Everything God does is Decent and in Order,
and we ought to be in that order!

NOTES

REVIEW OF MID-TERM

DISCIPLINE POSITION
"I Corinthians 15:58"

It is difficult to make it thru our daily life without discipline. When an individual does not have discipline their life, it can become chaotic. Chaotic to the point in which one does not complete anything in their life or it will get half-way done.

Discipline

- _____.
- _____
- _____
- _____
- _____

Strict- _____

- _____
- _____
- _____
- _____

Strengthens- _____.

- _____
- _____
- _____
- _____

- _____

- _____

Ways- _____

- _____

- _____

- _____

- _____

- _____

- _____

- _____

- ■ Progress: _____

  ○ _____

System- _____
_____

- _____

- _____

- _____

Self- _____

- _____

- _____

Control- _____

_____

- _____

- _____

- _____

- _____

Obedience- _____

_____

- _____

Training- _____

- _____
_____

- _____
_____

- _____
_____

- _____
_____
_____

LEADERSHIP RESPONSIBLITIES

When it comes to Discipline in Leadership (The practice of training people to obey rules, or a code of behavior.

Synonyms: _____

_____

Disciplines of a Pastor

Purity: _____

_____

- _____

- _____

Faithful: _____

_____

- _____

Relationship: _____

_____

- _____

Mind: _____

_____

- _____

Devotion: _____

Biblical Insight – Student's Manual

- _____

- _____

Integrity: _____
_____

- _____

Discipleship: _____
_____
_____

Project 11

1.) Know the meaning of Discipline
2.) Why should a leader be discipline?
3.) Are you Disciplined in your life, as well as, Ministry? Why?
4.) How will Discipline assist you in your life, as well as, Ministry?
5.) What are the six Disciplines of a Leader? Why?

Lets take a look at *I Corinthians 15:58*

_____
_____
_____
_____

- _____
_____

- _____
  _____

- _____
  _____

Discipline will bring an individual to continueth in their Beliefs, Assignments, and even Mission, especially when it becomes a way of their life.

Furthermore, when an individual applies Discipline to their life then it will be Saturated into their Heart, in order, for the person to have a Discipline Position.

Wow! Now you have a Position…….

❖ The question is are you ready for the position?

One may say, "Ready for what Position"? Looking at "Position" which is when, a person will hold or even stand in, for a given season and/or seasons, to labor in for the Kingdom of God.

Certainly, there are different kinds of Position, and another name for "_____
_____".

Some Positions have little Responsibilities, Much or even Greater Responsibilities. No matter what your Position is you should be:

- ○ _____

- ○ _____

- ○ _____

- ○ _____

- ○ _____

When God calls you _____

_____

_____

➢ _____

_____

➢ _____

_____

➢ _____

_____

➢ _____

_____

➢ _____

_____

This is why in the first Section and your first assignment was "Time With God". He is the ONE who did Predestinate, Called, Qualify, and justified you for His Glory!!
_____.

The Position or Positions, in which, the Good Lord has equipped you for is a Divine One, for "Such a Time As This".

No matter what the Position is small or great. One MUST be Serious to maintain the Office in which the God of Host has placed an individual in. ____

_____

Whatever you do, do Not Neglect the Call of your Duty. No matter if your call of Duty is before people or behind closed doors. God is watching and He will Repay and Reward an individual with their works, no matter if it is good or bad. _____

_____

If you Neglect your Call of Duty, in which, the Good Lord above had given you. He can remove you if He chooses to. It is an Honor to be Chosen by God. He could had passed you by, however, He did not. Therefore, give your very best and Watch the Living God work for you on your behalf.

Furthermore, God will get all the Glory!!!!

PROTOCOL

The God, in which, we serve is a God of Order. He is a God of Order in all area of an individual's life. Protocol in the body of Christ is essential for the functioning of each service.

However, I am speaking of the Order pertaining to His Church or Ministries.

In which the Main Focus is the Living God and Winning Many Souls for Him. _____

_____

Protocol is _____

_____

_____

Without Protocol _____

_____

Each service should be _____

_____

Each service should have _____

_____

Lets make this Clear, _____

_____

There is an Understand which Compasses All Understanding and it is the "Peace of God", believe this only Few Individuals has this kind of "PEACE". No one can give you this Peace accept the Living God.

When an individual is serving in a Church or Ministry, especially as a Leader, _____
_____
_____

Most of all, _____
_____

A Leader should maintain, on a regular bases, a system (Time) to commune with the Highest, for Divine Directions in their (daily) walk with God. Especially, on Leading the People of God who are Precious in His sight!

LEADER

Indirectly (Not Face to Face)	**Directly (Face to Face)**

A Leader must be _____
_____

There are many different qualities, in which a Leader should have, such as knowledge, wisdom, and most of all understanding with Love to assist the people of God, in leading them in the ways of the Almighty.

➢ _____:

" _____

_____

_____

_____ "

➢ _____

_____

_____

_____

➢ _____

_____

_____

_____

_____

_____

_____

King Solomon had watched his father through-out his reign of forty years. And realized he needed much more in his spirit, to be able to reign with maturity and balance.

Know how to set up Church/Organization with different Ministries, Offices, Positions:

Along with their Duties and Responsibilities in which the Position calls for to maintain.

➢ Apostle> _____
_____
_____

➢ _____
_____
_____
_____.

➢ Bishop> _____
_____.

- Senior Pastor> _____
  _____

- Assistance Pastor> _____
  _____

- Associate Pastor> _____
  _____

- Prophet> _____
  _____.

- Teacher> _____
  _____.

- Evangelist> _____
  _____

- Youth Pastor> _____
  _____.

- Minister> _____
  _____.

- Armour bearer> _____
  _____

- Deacon/Deaconess> _____
  _____
  _____

- ➤ Treasurer> _____
  _____

- ➤ Secretary> _____
  _____.

- ➤ Ushers> _____
  _____

- ➤ Missionaries> _____
  _____
  _____.

- ➤ Choir> _____
  _____.

Project 12

(This project will demonstrate your wisdom/knowledge as a leader). See Companion Book for Section 1 Biblical Insights Projects.

    1.) Scenarios Eight (See hand out)

    2.) Careful read and analyze each scenario

One can never get enough of learning. This is why an individual should always have a teachable mindset. In as much as to stay Humble too.

Humility, will take you, where nothing else can. God tells us to walk Humbly, in His Word, before Him.

On the other hand, one should ask God for Common Sense, especially when it comes to Protocol, in order to know when to move, what to say and what not to say. Especially, when you are visiting another Church or Organization in Ministry.

The Good Lord will assist you with All your
Endeavors concerning the Ministry or Organization
in which
He has Entrusted you with!

CEREMONIES

There are times in which a group of individuals will come together in order to celebrate, unite, to be installed/ license/ ordain, or even saying final good-byes to a loved one or special friend.

This is consisted to be Ceremonies (A formal Religious or public occasion, typically celebrates particular events or anniversaries).

The major ceremonies that comes to mind are:

Each one of these services has a unique tone to it, in which, the participants are very proud, as well as, honor to be a part of.

It is vital in which every Leader should know how and why to perform each service, even if he/she has only conducted the ceremony one time.

All of these are to be conducted with dignity and decorum.

The conducting of these ceremonies are to be done in a timely matter.

Being on time is important, it will allow for any sudden change to a service or ceremony which <u>Must</u> be addressed, due to some unforeseen circumstances.

- In the case of Funerals and Weddings where in most cases time is _____
_____
_____
_____.

Some families might not want a long service. Some families request that the Service is in your hands and allow you to have the autonomy to as you see fit. _____

_____

_____

_____

_____

_____

- All the other ceremonies the same applies, you might not know what you may run into. Therefore, _____

_____

_____

_____

_____

_____

_____

_____.

One reference book, <u>Every</u> Minister should have in their possession is:

   "The Star Book for Ministers" by <u>Edward T. Hiscox</u>.

There are other "Minister's" Resource Books for conducting various ceremonies.

Ceremonies

Wedding

Is a ceremony, in which, the legally or formally recognized union of (2) people as partners in a personal relationship, between a Man and a Woman. Marriage is an institution with of GOD, and has ordained in the time of man's innocence, before he had sinned against His Maker, and been yet banish from Paradise.

There are Formal, Traditional, and laid-back Weddings with fun Themes, such as: Religious, Interfaith, Humanist, Non-Denominational, and Civil.

Each State in the United States has different Laws in placed for a Wedding Ceremony to be performed or Officiated.

For instance, in the State of Ohio a Minister Must be License or Ordained. The Minister should submit a Marriage Application at the State Level, to the Marriage Licensing Office at the Secretary of State.

- Ohio Secretary of State Minister's License
  "PO Box 1658, Columbus, Ohio 43216
  (614)728-9200

- Visit online to get a Classic Wedding Package and Registration with the State.

Responsibly of Minister

o _____

o _____ :

- _____
  _____

- _____
  _____

- _____
  _____

-
-
-
-
-

- Moving Forward:
  -
  -
  -
  -
  -

Dr. Eugenia Gumm & Elder Charles R. Byrd

- Performing the Wedding:
  - _____:
    - _____
    - _____.
    - _____
    - _____
    - _____
    - _____
    - _____
    - _____
    - _____
    - _____

○ _____
_____
○ _____
_____
○ _____
_____
○ _____
_____
○ _____
_____
○ _____
_____.

Project 13

1.) What is the first line of duty to do before you perform a Wedding?
2.) Should a Minister be licensed before performing a Wedding? Why?
3.) Why should a couple be counsel before getting married?
4.) Should a couple make sure he/she is ready for marriage? Why?
5.) What Scriptures should a Minister use to perform a Wedding?
6.) Should a Minister assist in preparing for a Wedding? Why?
7.) Should a Minister know how long a Wedding ceremony is to be performed? Why?

Baptism

_____

_____

_____

Baptize- _____.

Jesus was Baptized, _____
_____

The Word of God states,

"_____
_____"

Basically, this is saying, born of the water (which is being fully submerge in water), to be buried with Christ, as well as, enjoined with Him.

"_____
_____"

Being born _____
_____
_____

By making sure the individuals know the purpose for being Baptized and receiving the Holy Ghost _____
_____
_____
_____

Procedure for Baptism

❖ _____ :

- _____
   _____ .

- _____
   _____ .

- _____
   _____ .

- _____
   _____ .

These clothes _____
_____
_____

If a Church or Organization is _____
_____ .

See Example:

ABC Church/Organization
123 PO Box
Leafy, Ohio 1111

Baptism Permission Form

I _____ (Parent/Guardian), gives permission for _____ (Child), to be Baptized on _____ day, in the month of _____, 2020.

Performed by ABC Church/Organization

Baptized by: Apostle Elder Charles Byrd

- ❖ _____
  _____
  _____
  _____

- ❖ (See the book for Minister's:, "Star Book", mentioned at the beginning of this Chapter or "Minister's Handbook").

- ❖ Totally, Submerge the individual in water _____
  _____

- ❖ Once the individual comes up you can _____
  _____.

- ❖ Encourage the individual to praise the Lord for the person _____
  _____
  _____
  _____

❖ Once the individual is getting dress or finish with the Baptism. You can give them a Certificate of Baptism. (You can design the Certificate or purchase at online or a Christian Store).

Example of Baptism Certificate:

CERTIFICATE OF BAPTISM

This Certifies that
JOHN DOE

Was Baptized by Immersion in the NAME OF JESUS CHRIST OUR LORD on this 1ST Day of May, 2020 at ImPact Bible Academy, Dayton, Ohio 45417.

Officiated By Apostle Elder Charles R. Byrd

"Then Peter said unto them, Repent, and be Baptized every one of you in the Name of Jesus Christ for the remission of sins, and ye shall receive the gift of the Holy Ghost." *Acts 2:38*

_____   _____
Apostle Dr. Eugenia Gumm   Apostle Elder Charles R. Byrd

Project 14 Baptism

1.) Know the meaning of Baptism
2.) Know why a person should be Baptized
3.) Know the Scriptures for Baptism
4.) How old should a child be to be Baptism? Why?
5.) Does a child need to have a permission slip to be Baptize?
6.) Is there special clothing for Baptism? If there is, then name the clothing (Items).
7.) Conduct a Baptism Service

Funerals

- _____
  _____

- Discuss an Itinerary and order of service
    - _____
    - _____
    - _____
    - _____
    - _____
    - _____

- Procedure of Service
    - _____
    - _____

- _____

- _____

- _____
  _____

- _____
  _____
  _____

- _____
  _____
  _____

- _____
  _____
  _____
  _____

Project 15 Funeral

1.) Do you have to be License as a Minister to conduct a funeral?
2.) What is the first line of duty would you do when asked to do a funeral? Why?
3.) Do you have to know the family to do a funeral?
4.) Do you know what Scriptures to use for a funeral?
5.) Do you know how long to conduct a funeral?
6.) Should there be an order of service when doing a funeral? Why?
7.) Conduct a funeral service (From beginning to finish).

Project 16 Communion

In the Church world is when the service of Communion with our Lord and Savior Jesus Christ by the Lord's Supper, in which, the partaking of Bread (which is the body of Christ) and Wine (which is the blood of Christ).

By partaking of the Holy Communion often will show the Lord's death until He come back for His bride.

The Lord's Supper is sacred and should not be taken lightly. Therefore, a person should examine himself/herself to see if he/she is worthy to partake of the Lord's Supper.

By examining oneself by means of:

1.) _____
_____
_____

2.) _____
_____
_____
_____

3.) _____
_____
_____

4.) _____
_____
_____

After you had examined yourself then you can freely partake of the Lord's Supper, in which, you are worthy to join in!

The Course of Action (The Lord's Supper)

- _____
- _____
- _____
- _____
- _____
- _____
- _____
- _____
- _____

Demonstration of the Lord's Supper

1.) Know the meaning/History of taking the Lord's Supper
2.) Know the Scriptures associated with the Lord's Supper
3.) Should anyone partake of the Lord's Supper? Why?
4.) Is the Lord's Supper important? Why?
5.) Know how to conduct the Lord's Supper?

The four ceremonies previously mentioned are in this first section "Biblical Insights". The remaining ceremonies listed in the beginning of this chapter with be discuss in Sections two, three, and four.

May the knowledge of these lessons increase you more and more in God's Word for ever and ever, Amen!

May the Good Lord Above Continueth to take you Higher and Higher!!!!

In the Glory of the Most High God!

REVIEW FINAL TEST

REFERENCES

Hiscox, E. T. (1878). *The Star Book For Ministers*. Prussia, PA: Judson Press. (Used by Permission)

King James Bible

Knight, G. W.; Ray, W. R. (2005). *The Illustrated Bible Dictionary*. Uhrichsville, OH: Barbour Publishing, Inc. (Used by Permission)

McQuade, P. L., Kent, P. (2009). *The Dictionary of Bible Names* (1st Edition). Uhrichsville, OH: Barbour Publishing, Inc. (Used by Permission)

Merriam-Webster Children's Dictionary, (2000) (First American Edition). London, England: Dorling Kindersley. (Used by Permission)

Strong, J.,LL.D, S.T.D. (2010). *The New Strong's Expanded Exhaustive Concordance of the Bible*. Nashville, TN: Thomas Nelson Publishing. (Used by Permission)

Webster's New World College Dictionary, (2002) (Fourth Edition). Hoboken, New Jersey: Wiley Publishing, Inc. (Used by Permission)

www.ingramcontent.com/pod-product-compliance
Lightning Source LLC
Chambersburg PA
CBHW081355230426
43667CB00017B/2843